I0143145

Faith That Moves the World

Also by Philip Hutchings

A Mouthful of Miracles

Faith That Moves the World

Faith That Moves the World

*Unlocking the Power to Live, Overcome, and
See God Move*

Philip Hutchings

Rise UP

Without limiting the rights under copyright(s) reserved below, no part of this publication may be reproduced, stored in or introduced into a retrieval system, or transmitted, in any form, or by any means (electronic, mechanical, photocopying, recording, or otherwise) without the prior permission of the publisher and the copyright owner.

The content of this book is provided "AS IS." The Publisher and the Author make no guarantees or warranties as to the accuracy, adequacy or completeness of or results to be obtained from using the content of this book, including any information that can be accessed through hyperlinks or otherwise, and expressly disclaim any warranty expressed or implied, including but not limited to implied warranties of merchantability or fitness for a particular purpose. This limitation of liability shall apply to any claim or cause whatsoever whether such claim or cause arises in contract, tort, or otherwise. In short, you, the reader, are responsible for your choices and the results they bring.

The scanning, uploading, and distributing of this book via the internet or via any other means without the permission of the publisher and copyright owner is illegal and punishable by law. Please purchase only authorized copies, and do not participate in or encourage piracy of copyrighted materials. Your support of the author's rights is appreciated.

Unless otherwise indicated, Scripture quotations are taken from the Amplified® Bible, Classic Edition . Copyright © 1954, 1958, 1962, 1964, 1965, 1987 by The Lockman Foundation. Used by permission. All rights reserved. (www.Lockman.org)

Scripture quotations marked (KJV) are taken from the King James Version of the Bible. Public domain.

Copyright © 2025 by Higher Life Church. All rights reserved under International and Pan-American Copyright Conventions.

Contents

Introduction

Every believer reaches a point in their life where they must ask themselves: "What do I really believe?"

In a world of noise, pressure, and compromise, your answer to that question will determine everything. THIS BOOK WILL HIT THAT! And it's not just a collection of teachings —it's really a call to arms. A call to rise up in faith. A call to kill fear, to reject passivity, and to walk in the fullness of what Jesus Christ died to give you. Whether you're a new Christian or a Spirit-filled veteran, you're going to see your faith go to a new level.

Faith is not just a doctrine. It's not a denomination. It's not a buzzword. Faith is the lifestyle of the Kingdom. Without it, you cannot be saved. Without it, you cannot please God. Without it, you cannot overcome.

In these pages, we're going to walk through what faith is, what it's not, where it comes from, how to build it, how to release it, and how to live by it—especially in these last days. This is a manual for victory; a blueprint for believers, who are done with being tossed around by doubt and fear. It's for those who are ready to become dangerous to the Devil and useful to the Kingdom. If you'll receive it, and if you'll apply it, this book will ignite your spirit and shift your life.

Because when you believe God—everything changes.

Let's go.

Chapter One

Why Does Faith Matter?

F aith is not a side topic in the Kingdom of God—it is the very foundation. From the beginning of creation to the smallest breakthrough in your life, FAITH is the activating force. Faith is not a suggestion; it is a requirement.

> As Jesus went into Capernaum, a centurion came up
>   to Him, begging Him,
> And saying, Lord, my servant boy is lying at the
>   house paralyzed *and* distressed with intense pains.
> And Jesus said to him, I will come and restore him.
> But the centurion replied to Him, Lord, I am not
>   worthy *or* fit to have You come under my roof; but
>   only speak the word, and my servant boy will be
>   cured.
> For I also am a man subject to authority, with soldiers
>   subject to me. And I say to one, Go, and he goes;
>   and to another, Come, and he comes; and to my
>   slave, Do this, and he does it.
> When Jesus heard him, He marveled and said to

those who followed Him [who adhered steadfastly
to Him, conforming to His example in living and,
if need be, in dying also], I tell you truly, I have
not found so much faith as this with anyone, even
in Israel.

I tell you, many will come from east and west, and
will sit at table with Abraham, Isaac, and Jacob in
the kingdom of heaven,

While the sons *and* heirs of the kingdom will be
driven out into the darkness outside, where there
will be weeping and grinding of teeth.

Then to the centurion Jesus said, Go; it shall be done
for you as you have believed. And the servant boy
was restored to health at that very moment.

— Matthew 8:5–13

As Jesus passed on from there, two blind men
followed Him, shouting loudly, Have
pity *and* mercy on us, Son of David!

When He reached the house and went in, the blind
men came to Him, and Jesus said to them, Do you
believe that I am able to do this? They said to
Him, Yes, Lord.

Then He touched their eyes, saying, According to
your faith *and* trust *and* reliance [on the power
invested in Me] be it done to you;

And their eyes were opened. And Jesus
earnestly *and* sternly charged them, See that you
let no one know about this.

But they went off and blazed *and* spread His fame
abroad throughout that whole district.

— Matthew 9:27–31

Now faith is the assurance (the confirmation, the title
deed) of the things [we] hope for, being the proof
of things [we] do not see *and* the conviction of
their reality [faith perceiving as real fact what is
not revealed to the senses].

For by [faith—trust and holy fervor born of faith] the
men of old had divine testimony borne to
them *and* obtained a good report.

By faith we understand that the worlds [during the
successive ages] were framed (fashioned, put in
order, and equipped for their intended purpose)
by the word of God, so that what we see was not
made out of things which are visible.

[Prompted, actuated] by faith Abel brought God a
better and more acceptable sacrifice than Cain,
because of which it was testified of him that he
was righteous [that he was upright and in right
standing with God], and God bore witness by
accepting *and* acknowledging his gifts. And
though he died, yet [through the incident] he is
still speaking.

Because of faith Enoch was caught up *and* transferred
to heaven, so that he did not have a glimpse of
death; and he was not found, because God had
translated him. For even before he was taken to

> heaven, he received testimony [still on record]
> that he had pleased *and* been satisfactory to God.
But without faith it is impossible to please *and* be
> satisfactory to Him. For whoever would come
> near to God must [necessarily] believe that God
> exists and that He is the rewarder of those who
> earnestly *and* diligently seek Him [out].

> — Hebrews 11:1–6

Faith is the substance, the assurance, the title deed of things hoped for. It is the evidence of what we do not yet see. Verse 6 makes it clear: without faith, it is impossible to please God. That's not optional; that's a divine mandate. Faith isn't just a tool for receiving—it's the method by which the very world was formed. By faith, we understand that the universe was framed by the Word of God (Hebrews 11:3). That tells us something crucial: faith gave birth to the most outstanding exploit in existence—creation.

> For whatever is born of God is victorious over the
> world; and this is the victory that conquers the
> world, even our faith.

> — 1 John 5:4

What is faith worth? *Everything.*

Faith is what overcomes the world. Not grit. Not good behavior. Not popularity, but rather FAITH.

settle this: Every outstanding event in a person's life in u. Kingdom will result from their faith. Even entry into the Kingdom—getting born again—is by faith. "For by grace are you saved through faith" (Ephesians 2:8). Your future in the Kingdom is not Devil-determined. It's not even God-determined in the way many think. Until you believe, God cannot perform.

As David Oyedepo[1] said, "What you become is a function of what you believe. Everything about your life is faith-determined."

If God uses faith in all that He does, so should we. Be imitators of God, as dearly loved children (Ephesians 5:1). And I believe that's why I heard the Holy Spirit clearly say, "Teach them faith." That's the mandate.

Matthew 8:17 says, "*And thus He fulfilled what was spoken by the prophet Isaiah, He Himself took [in order to carry away] our weaknesses and infirmities and bore away our diseases.*" And Matthew 9:29 says, "*Then He touched their eyes, saying, According to your faith and trust and reliance [on the power invested in Me] be it done to you.*"

When you reread the verses above, do you notice anything? Time and again, Jesus points to faith as the determining factor.

Faith is the key that unlocks Heaven's storehouse. Faith changes everything it touches. Faith invites God into your

---

1. David Oyedepo is the founding bishop of Living Faith Church Worldwide (also known as Winners' Chapel), based in Nigeria. He is widely recognized as a leading voice in the Word of Faith

situation. There is no limit to what faith can do—except the limits we put on it. Faith does not recognize the word "impossible." It empowers you to become anything the Word says. It empowers you to have, to do, and to overcome.

Habakkuk 2:4; Romans 1:17; Galatians 3:11; Hebrews 10:38: All say, *"The just shall live by faith."*

That's not a suggestion—it's a victory strategy. Everything in the Kingdom requires faith to actualize. And in this final chapter of human history, faith is not just important—it's essential.

Faith is how we see God move.

Faith is how we live.

Faith is how we overcome.

Chapter Two

What Is Faith—and What It's Not

F aith is the ability to believe God—without demanding proof. It's not rooted in evidence, logic, or the five senses. Faith believes simply because of trust in the One who spoke.

> Now faith is the assurance (the confirmation, the title deed) of the things [we] hope for, being the proof of things [we] do not see and the conviction of their reality [faith perceiving as real fact what is not revealed to the senses].
>
> — Hebrews 11:1

Faith is the confidence that what we hope for will actually happen. It's not wishful thinking—it's spiritual substance. It reaches into the unseen and pulls God's promises into the visible world. Faith is spiritual eyesight. It sees with the heart when the eyes can't see anything. It's a heart-rooted conviction, not a mind-based opinion.

As it is written, I have made you the father of many
nations. [He was appointed our father] in the
sight of God in Whom he believed, Who gives life
to the dead and speaks of the nonexistent things
that [He has foretold and promised] as if they
[already] existed.

[For Abraham, human reason for] hope being gone,
hoped in faith that he should become the father of
many nations, as he had been promised, So [num-
berless] shall your descendants be.

He did not weaken in faith when he considered the
[utter] impotence of his own body, which was as
good as dead because he was about a hundred
years old, or [when he considered] the barrenness
of Sarah's [deadened] womb.

No unbelief *or* distrust made him waver (doubtingly
question) concerning the promise of God, but he
grew strong *and* was empowered by faith as he
gave praise *and* glory to God,

Fully satisfied *and* assured that God was
able *and* mighty to keep His word *and* to do what
He had promised.

— Romans 4:17–21

Wow!

Abraham is our example. He believed in the promise when
it made no natural sense. He didn't consider the physical
evidence—he considered the promise of God. Faith is not a
product of reasoning. It doesn't come from your five senses.

In fact, when you start leaning into your senses and emotions, you begin to drift out of faith and into fear. And fear always compromises the Word.

Faith and fear operate the same way—but in opposite directions.

When you meditate on God's Word, faith grows. When you meditate on fear, it becomes a stronghold too—but a destructive one. Faith does not come from what we feel—it comes from what God said. That's why Paul says, *"We walk by faith, not by sight"* 2 Corinthians 5:7. Faith walks by what God has declared, not what man has reported.

Let's talk about the contrast.

Thomas Faith says, "Unless I see it, I won't believe it."

Abraham Faith says, "I'm fully persuaded because God said it."

Too many believers are walking in head faith instead of heart faith. Head faith agrees with God's Word but doesn't act on it. It's merely mental assent. It acknowledges, "Yes, that's true," yet lives as if it's not. Heart faith believes and responds.

It moves.

It confesses.

It obeys.

So then faith cometh by hearing, and hearing by the
  word of God.

— Romans 10:17 (KJV)

The Word is the only true source of faith. It's neither hype
nor emotion. It's the living Word of God.

My son, attend to my words; consent *and* submit to
  my sayings.
Let them not depart from your sight; keep them in
  the center of your heart.
For they are life to those who find them,
  healing *and* health to all their flesh.

— Proverbs 4:20–22

Whatever has your focus determines your future. What you
consistently listen to shapes your faith. Faith comes by
hearing—but grows through meditation. Faith is more than
just agreeing with God. It's behaving as if what He said is
final, regardless of circumstances.

Chapter Three

Where Does Faith Come From?

F aith doesn't appear out of thin air. It has a source, and the Bible makes it clear: *"Faith comes by hearing, and hearing by the Word of God"* (Romans 10:17). The Word is the divine supply line. If faith is the fuel, then the Word is the fuel station. No Word—no faith. It's that simple.

Remember Proverbs 4:20–22? Whatever has your attention has your focus, and whatever has your focus shapes your future. If you give your attention to God's Word, faith will grow naturally. The Word of God is God's faith-filled speech. When you read it, meditate on it, and declare it, you receive the same substance that created the world. The source of faith is the Word.

And this faith is not man-made—it is God's own faith. It's supernatural. It's alive. And it's powerful.

Go back and reread Romans 4:17–21. Abraham didn't believe in some vague, spiritual idea; he believed the Word of the Lord. He was fully convinced that God was both able and faithful to fulfill what He had promised. He understood that when God speaks, it's a done deal.

Faith is being fully convinced. That kind of faith doesn't come from wishing or wanting; it comes from feeding on the Word until your heart is anchored, steady, and unshakable. Faith doesn't begin with your circumstances—it begins with your convictions, and convictions come from the Word.

Chapter Four

Building Your Faith

Y ou don't just get faith—you build it.

Faith can be cultivated, strengthened, and grown. Like a muscle, it responds to use. The building process begins with one powerful instruction:

Be strong (confident) and of good courage, for you
shall cause this people to inherit the land which I
swore to their fathers to give them.
Only you be strong and very courageous, that you
may do according to all the law which Moses My
servant commanded you. Turn not from it to the
right hand or to the left, that you may prosper
wherever you go.
This Book of the Law shall not depart out of your
mouth, but you shall meditate on it day and night,
that you may observe *and* do according to all that
is written in it. For then you shall make your way

prosperous, and then you shall deal
wisely *and* have good success.
Have not I commanded you? Be strong, vigorous, and
very courageous. Be not afraid, neither be
dismayed, for the Lord your God is with you
wherever you go.

— Joshua 1:6–9

"Meditate on My Word day and night…" Why?

Because meditation is how faith takes root. It's not enough
to read the Word; you have to sit with it, turn it over in your
heart, speak it, and chew on it. That's where faith begins to
grow. Meditation creates a stronghold of faith. It's just like
digestion: your body breaks down food and sends nutrients
to the areas that need energy. Meditation breaks down the
Word and sends faith and power to the areas of your life
that need strength. Faith without meditation is like seed
without soil—it won't take root.

And He said to them, Do you not discern *and* under-
stand this parable? How then is it possible for you
to discern *and* understand all the parables?
The sower sows the Word.
The ones along the path are those who have the
Word sown [in their hearts], but when they hear,
Satan comes at once and [by force] takes away the
message which is sown in them.
And in the same way the ones sown upon stony

ground are those who, when they hear the Word,
at once receive *and* accept *and* welcome it with joy;

And they have no real root in themselves, and so they
endure for a little while; then when trouble or
persecution arises on account of the Word, they
immediately are offended (become displeased,
indignant, resentful) *and* they stumble *and* fall
away.

And the ones sown among the thorns are others who
hear the Word;

Then the cares *and* anxieties of the world *and* distrac-
tions of the age, and the
pleasure *and* delight *and* false glamour *and* deceit-
fulness of riches, and the craving *and* passionate
desire for other things creep in and
choke *and* suffocate the Word, and it becomes
fruitless.

And those sown on the good (well-adapted) soil are
the ones who hear the Word and
receive *and* accept *and* welcome it and bear fruit—
some thirty times as much as was sown, some
sixty times as much, and some [even] a hundred
times as much.

— Mark 4:13–20

Without roots, faith cannot survive pressure, persecution,
or delay.

And FAITH has levels:

- No Faith
- Little Faith
- Great Faith

The determining factor is depth—not how many scriptures you quote, but how convinced you are of the ones you do.

> The apostles said to the Lord, Increase our faith (that trust and confidence that spring from our belief in God).
> And the Lord answered, If you had faith (trust and confidence in God) even [so small] like a grain of mustard seed, you could say to this mulberry tree, Be pulled up by the roots, and be planted in the sea, and it would obey you.
>
> — Luke 17:5–6

The disciples didn't ask for miracles. They asked Jesus, *"Increase our faith."* They understood that more faith meant more breakthrough. Depth of conviction moves Heaven. One scripture, fully believed, can change your life.

Some examples come to my mind:

1. Kenneth Hagin[1] rose from a deathbed on Mark 11:23.
2. John G. Lake[2] built a healing movement on Acts 10:38.

You don't need a multitude of verses—you need deep roots. In Genesis 1:3 – God said one word, and light came. He didn't repeat it. Stop chasing volume. Start pursuing depth.

Build your faith. Grab the Word. Meditate on it. Let it sink deep. Let it form unshakable conviction. Because conviction is what produces miracles.

---

1. Kenneth E. Hagin (1917–2003) was a prominent American Pentecostal preacher and teacher, widely regarded as a founding figure of the Word of Faith movement. He established Rhema Bible Training College in Broken Arrow, Oklahoma, and authored numerous books on faith, healing, and spiritual authority.
2. John G. Lake (1870–1935) was a Canadian-American Pentecostal minister and missionary known for his healing ministry and strong emphasis on the power of the Holy Spirit. He founded healing rooms in Spokane, Washington, and played a significant role in the early Pentecostal movement, particularly through his missionary work in South Africa and his teachings on divine healing and spiritual authority.

Chapter Five

Fear—Faith's Enemy

L et's get this straight: You're always operating either in faith or fear. Every decision, every response, every word—you're either moving in faith or in fear. There's no neutral ground. And here's the truth: fear is compromised faith. It's faith in reverse. It's still belief—but it's belief in the wrong outcome.

Think back to Mark 4:13–20 in the previous chapter.

When you allow other voices to dominate your thinking, you begin to turn left and right instead of remaining centered on the Word. Jesus said that without roots, faith withers when pressure comes. Fear doesn't just happen; it grows in the same way that faith does—by hearing. Hearing the contradiction. Hearing the opinions of your senses. Hearing the bad reports.

Reread Romans 4.

Abraham didn't consider the externals. That's why his faith held steady.

Fear becomes a stronghold through meditation—just like faith.

"As a man thinks in his heart, so is he" Proverbs 23:7.

When you meditate on what fear is telling you, it breaks down and infiltrates every area of your life. It becomes a system in your soul, shutting things down. Fear, when believed and acted upon, produces the law of sin and death. It makes you live like someone without God—even when you're born again. Fear is not natural for a believer; it's like breathing underwater—it doesn't belong in your new nature.

Read Numbers 13–14. There were twelve spies. Ten walked in fear. Two walked in faith.

God said, "You can take the land." They said, "We can't." One day of wrong confession equaled one year of wilderness wandering. It wasn't the giants in Canaan that kept them out—it was the giants in their hearts. Their mouths revealed what was really inside them.

Are you faith-filled or faith in reverse?

Fear will hijack your calling. It will make you settle for Ishmael when God promised Isaac. It will cause you to force something in the flesh and then blame God when it doesn't work. Stop calling fear "wisdom." Just because it sounds cautious doesn't mean it's Spirit-led.

I declare your time for settling ends now.

Don't let fear hijack your:

- Perspective
- Words
- Actions
- Destiny

If you're going to doubt anything, doubt your doubts. God has never failed. Don't let fear call Him a liar.

Compare Luke 1:8–20 with Luke 1:26–38.

> Now while on duty, serving as priest before God in the order of his division,
>
> As was the custom of the priesthood, it fell to him by lot to enter [the sanctuary of] the temple of the Lord and burn incense.
>
> And all the throng of people were praying outside [in the court] at the hour of incense [burning].
>
> And there appeared to him an angel of the Lord, standing at the right side of the altar of incense.
>
> And when Zachariah saw him, he was troubled, and fear took possession of him.
>
> But the angel said to him, Do not be afraid, Zachariah, because your petition was heard, and your wife Elizabeth will bear you a son, and you must call his name John [God is favorable].
>
> And you shall have joy and exultant delight, and many will rejoice over his birth,
>
> For he will be great *and* distinguished in the sight of the Lord. And he must drink no wine nor strong

drink, and he will be filled with *and* controlled by
the Holy Spirit even in *and* from his mother's
womb.

And he will turn back *and* cause to return many of the
sons of Israel to the Lord their God,

And he will [himself] go before Him in the spirit and
power of Elijah, to turn back the hearts of the
fathers to the children, and the
disobedient *and* incredulous *and* unpersuadable to
the wisdom of the upright [which is the knowledge and holy love of the will of God]—in order to
make ready for the Lord a people [perfectly]
prepared [in spirit, adjusted and disposed and
placed in the right moral state].

And Zachariah said to the angel, By what shall I
know *and* be sure of this? For I am an old man,
and my wife is well advanced in years.

And the angel replied to him, I am Gabriel. I stand in
the [very] presence of God, and I have been sent
to talk to you and to bring you this good news.

Now behold, you will be *and* will continue to be silent
and not able to speak till the day when these
things take place, because you have not believed
what I told you; but my words are of a kind which
will be fulfilled in the appointed *and* proper time.

— Luke 1:8-20

Now in the sixth month [after that], the angel
Gabriel was sent from God to a town of Galilee
named Nazareth,

To a girl never having been married *and* a virgin
engaged to be married to a man whose name was
Joseph, a descendant of the house of David; and
the virgin's name was Mary.

And he came to her and said, Hail, O favored one
[endued with grace]! The Lord is with you! *Blessed*
(favored of God) are you before all other women!

But *when she saw him*, she was greatly
troubled *and* disturbed *and* confused at what he
said and kept revolving in her mind what such a
greeting might mean.

And the angel said to her, Do not be afraid, Mary, for
you have found grace (free, spontaneous, absolute
favor and loving-kindness) with God.

And listen! You will become pregnant and will give
birth to a Son, and you shall call His name Jesus.

He will be great (eminent) and will be called the Son
of the Most High; and the Lord God will give to
Him the throne of His forefather David,

And He will reign over the house of Jacob throughout
the ages; and of His reign there will be no end.

And Mary said to the angel, How can this be, since I
have no [intimacy with any man as a] husband?

Then the angel said to her, The Holy Spirit will come
upon you, and the power of the Most High will
overshadow you [like a shining cloud]; and so the
holy (pure, sinless) Thing (Offspring) which shall
be born *of you* will be called the Son of God.

And listen! Your relative Elizabeth in her old age has
also conceived a son, and this is now the sixth
month with her who was called barren.

For with God nothing is ever impossible *and* no word from God shall be without power *or* impossible of fulfillment.

Then Mary said, Behold, I am the handmaiden of the Lord; let it be done to me according to what you have said. And the angel left her.

— Luke 1:26-38

Two people heard from God. One responded with doubt, while the other responded with faith. One lost his voice, whereas the other birthed the Savior.

What will your response be?

Chapter Six

Working Your Faith

You don't just *have* faith—you've got to *work* it.

Faith isn't passive. It's not a quiet belief tucked away in your heart. Faith is alive, active, and productive. It does something.

Faith empowers you to:

1. BECOME what the Word says
2. HAVE what the Word says
3. DO what the Word says

Everything in the Kingdom requires faith to function. It is the key to activating Kingdom realities.

Remember Habakkuk 2:4, Romans 1:17, Galatians 3:11, Hebrews 10:38: *"The just shall live by faith."* Not visit it occasionally—live by it. Faith is your daily lifestyle.

> And Jesus, replying, said to them, Have faith in God
> [constantly].
> Truly I tell you, whoever says to this mountain, Be
> lifted up and thrown into the sea! and does not
> doubt at all in his heart but believes that what he
> says will take place, it will be done for him.
> For this reason I am telling you, whatever you ask for
> in prayer, believe (trust and be confident) that it is
> granted to you, and you will [get it].

— Mark 11:22–24

Jesus said, *"Have faith in God."* Then He described what faith does—it speaks to the mountain and believes it's done.

Faith *talks*.

Faith *acts*.

Faith *expects*.

We cannot win in life with pop psychology, clever church programs, or feel-good sermons. It requires faith. Faith is still fresh. Still alive. Still powerful. It hasn't passed away—it's just been neglected. God is calling us back to what works. And faith works. Faith transforms everything it touches.

They said, "No one can kill Goliath."

Faith said, "Hand me a sling."

Faith can use the smallest thing to defeat the biggest obstacle. Faith doesn't recognize impossibility. It created the world—so everything in the world must respond to it. We are in the final days of history. And in this hour, faith is not just your edge—it's your lifeline. Knowing how to operate in faith is no longer optional; it is a matter of life and death.

Work your faith:

1. *Believe* the Word
2. *Speak* the Word
3. *Act* on the Word
4. *Expect* results

Because faith without works is dead—but faith with action is unstoppable.

Chapter Seven

Head vs. Heart Faith

Many people know the Bible, but few truly believe it. There's a massive difference between head faith and heart faith. One agrees with the truth; the other is convinced by it. One can quote Scripture, while the other lives Scripture. Head Faith says, "I know what the Bible says." Heart Faith says, "It is settled—no matter what I see or feel."

> But Thomas, one of the Twelve, called the Twin, was not with them when Jesus came.
>
> So the other disciples kept telling him, We have seen the Lord! But he said to them, Unless I see in His hands the marks made by the nails and put my finger into the nail prints, and put my hand into His side, I will never believe [it].
>
> Eight days later His disciples were again in the house, and Thomas was with them. Jesus came, though they were behind closed doors, and stood among them and said, Peace to you!

Then He said to Thomas, Reach out your finger here,
    and see My hands; and put out your hand and
    place [it] in My side. Do not be
    faithless *and* incredulous, but [stop your unbelief
    and] believe!
Thomas answered Him, My Lord and my God!
Jesus said to him, Because you have seen Me, *Thomas,*
    do you now believe (trust, have faith)?
    Blessed *and* happy *and* to be envied are those who
    have never seen Me and yet have
    believed *and* adhered to *and* trusted *and* relied
    on Me.

— John 20:24–29

Thomas knew Jesus. But he still wouldn't believe until he saw. That's head faith—based on the five senses. Don't forget Romans 4:17–21. Abraham didn't consider the natural. That's heart faith—anchored in the spirit. We were created for our spirit to lead our soul and body.

Spirit → Soul (mind, will, emotions) → Body

But after the fall, the order flipped. Even as born-again believers, our spirit can be trapped if it isn't fed the Word. In a moment of crisis, your soul will step aside and say to your spirit, "Do something!" But if your spirit has been starved, it stands there blank. There's nothing in there. Why? Because all you've deposited is fear, doubt, and reasoning.

Meditate on the Word. Let it drop from your head into your heart. If it remains in your head, your theology will shift with your tragedy. But if it's in your heart, your theology will transform the tragedy. John Wesley[1] once said that the Devil has given the church a substitute for faith—one that sounds so close, most can't tell the difference. It's called mental assent.

Some will say, "I know the Bible says that."

But they don't live like they believe it.

Only heart faith receives from God. You'll never understand God through feelings. Feelings are unreliable. Faith is based on the unchanging Word of God. Thomas relied on his senses, while Abraham focused on the promise. Which one are you? Heart faith is fully convinced. It believes without needing proof and moves beyond common sense into Scriptural sense. God's wisdom will often offend your natural logic, but it will produce supernatural results.

Stop letting your head talk your heart out of the promise. Move from head faith to heart faith—and watch God move.

---

1. John Wesley (1703–1791) was an Anglican cleric and theologian who, along with his brother Charles, founded Methodism. His teachings emphasized holiness, grace, and practical Christian living.

Chapter Eight

Releasing Your Faith

Faith that's only believed but never expressed is dormant. It's not enough to have faith in your heart—you must release it through your words and your actions.

> And there was a woman who had had a flow of blood for twelve years,
> And who had endured much suffering under [the hands of] many physicians and had spent all that she had, and was no better but instead grew worse.
> She had heard the reports concerning Jesus, and she came up behind Him in the throng and touched His garment,
> For she kept saying, If I only touch His garments, I shall be restored to health.

And immediately her flow of blood was dried up at
the source, and [suddenly] she felt in her body
that she was healed of her [distressing] ailment.

— Mark 5:25–29

The woman with the issue of blood had real, living faith.

How do we know?

She heard the Word.

She kept saying, "If I touch Him, I'll be healed."

She acted on what she believed.

She testified to the miracle.

This is how faith flows: Hearing → Speaking → Acting → Receiving

Faith is released by words. I'm going to keep reminding you about Romans 4:17: God calls things that be not as though they were. He framed the world with words. Jesus spoke to a fig tree—and it obeyed. When you speak in agreement with God, you're not just saying words; you're releasing faith.

Most people think of confession only as admitting sin. However, there's another side—confessing God's Word. Hebrews 3:1 calls Christianity the "Great Confession". *Confession* means "to say the same thing" as God.

I have believed, and therefore have I spoken.

— 2 Corinthians 4:13

This is the pattern: believe, then speak.

> For with the heart a person believes (adheres to,
> trusts in, and relies on Christ) and so is justified
> (declared righteous, acceptable to God), and with
> the mouth he confesses (declares openly and
> speaks out freely his faith) *and* confirms [his]
> salvation.

— Romans 10:10

Faith that remains unspoken is seen by God as an opinion—
not a conviction.

> A man's [moral] self shall be filled with the fruit of
> his mouth; and with the consequence of his words
> he must be satisfied [whether good or evil].
> Death and life are in the power of the tongue, and
> they who indulge in it shall eat the fruit of it [for
> death or life]

— Proverbs 18:20–21

> But I tell you, on the day of judgment men will have
> to give account for every idle (inoperative,
> nonworking) word they speak.
> For by your words you will be justified and acquitted,

and by your words you will be condemned and sentenced.

— Matthew 12:36–37

Your words frame your world. They are either building or undermining your future. They reveal what you truly believe. When you speak contrary to God's Word, you're in rebellion—just as disobedience is an action. God takes this seriously.

Your confession should center on five key truths:

1. What God accomplished for you through Christ.
2. What He has done in you through the new birth and Holy Spirit.
3. Who you are to God in Christ.
4. What Jesus is doing for you now at the right hand of the Father.
5. What God can do through you and your words.

Think back to Mark 11:22–24. Jesus backs His Word in your mouth. However, no sound equals no signs. Begin speaking His Word. Allow your confession to dispel fear and stir faith. Faith speaks. Faith acts. Faith receives.

> Bless (affectionately, gratefully praise) the Lord, O
>   my soul; and all that is [deepest] within me, bless
>   His holy name!
> Bless (affectionately, gratefully praise) the Lord, O
>   my soul, and forget not [one of] all His benefits—

Who forgives [every one of] all your iniquities, Who
    heals [each one of] all your diseases,
Who redeems your life from the pit and corruption,
    Who beautifies, dignifies, and crowns you with
    loving-kindness and tender mercy;
Who satisfies your mouth [your necessity and desire
    at your personal age and situation] with good so
    that your youth, renewed, is like the eagle's
    [strong, overcoming, soaring]!

— Psalm 103:1–5

Verse 5 says He fills your mouth with good "things." The Hebrew root of that word is "words." Why? Because words create things.

Faith activation checklist:

1. *Get* into the Word
2. *Meditate* on it
3. *Confess* it daily
4. *Act* on it boldly

Don't stop until your world reflects His Word—keep going.

Chapter Nine

Faith in the Final Hour

We are not living in normal times. The world is shaking. Systems are failing. Morality is crumbling. Truth is under attack. And in the midst of it all, God is calling for a people who will stand in faith. This is not the time for casual Christianity or comfortable church culture. This is the time for raw, unshakable, mountain-moving faith.

Faith is not optional. It's not just how we get saved; it's how we survive, overcome, and finish strong. When the pressure rises and the world gets darker, faith is your only way forward.

Pop psychology can't save you. Motivational quotes won't carry you through. Political leaders, government policies, and cultural movements can't fix the world. Only faith in the living God can anchor you.

In this final hour, faith is:

1. Your *shield*
2. Your *weapon*
3. Your *foundation*
4. Your *fuel*

Faith is your weapon. Use it to fight, build, stand, and move forward when everything around you urges you to quit.

God is preparing a remnant—a people who won't bow, who won't break, and who won't blend in. This message is not just theological; it is prophetic.

These people do not walk by sight. Fear cannot silence them. They will not abandon the promise.

They will live by faith, speak by faith, move by faith, and conquer by faith. These are the Daniels, the Deborahs, the Esthers, and the Elijahs of our time—people who hear God, believe Him, and move mountains by faith.

This is your moment. This is your hour. This is your faith. Don't shrink back. Don't lose heart. Live by faith—and finish strong.

Chapter Ten

Activate Your Faith (Challenge & Reflection)

Y ou've heard the Word. You've studied the principles. You've seen the power of faith through Scripture. Now, it's time to activate it. Faith without action is merely information; faith that is acted upon becomes revelation in motion.

Here's your challenge:

1. *Go* to the Word. Get a promise from God's Word that speaks directly to your situation.
2. *Meditate* on it. Sit with it. Speak it. Picture it. Let it sink deep. Let it become more real than what you see.
3. *Confess* it. Declare it with your mouth. Refuse to say anything contrary. Speak the end from the beginning.
4. *Act* on it. Take bold, practical steps in line with what you believe. Even if they feel small, take them in faith.

Read:

1. Mark 5:25–29 — the woman with the issue of blood
2. Joshua 6:2–20 — the walls of Jericho
3. James 1:22 — be doers of the Word
4. Matthew 7:24–27 — the wise man who built on the rock

Faith must be acted upon, or it's dead. If you're not ready to act, keep building until you are. But here's the key: start somewhere. Even a mustard seed of faith can move a mountain.

Also—don't forget this critical truth: Forgive. Unforgiveness is a faith blocker. Faith won't work in an unforgiving heart.

Faith Activation Exercise:

1. Identify your situation. What do you need God to move in?
2. Find a Scripture. What does God's Word say about it?
3. Write your confession. What will you declare about this situation based on God's Word?
4. Plan your action. What step of faith will you take this week to act on what you believe?
5. Do it—and don't back down. Faith works when you work it. Your words frame your world.

Let your confession reflect:

1. What God did for you in Christ

2. What He's done in you by His Spirit
3. Who you are in Him
4. What He's doing for you now
5. What He's about to do through you

"Teach them faith." That was my assignment. And now it's yours.

Don't just believe—activate.

Don't just know—move.

Don't just sit—speak and step.

Faith without action is dead, but faith with action changes everything.

Afterword

Faith for the Days Ahead

You've just read through ten chapters of foundational, biblical, Spirit-breathed truth about faith. However, none of this will benefit you if it remains simply words on a page. Now is the time to act.

We are not living in casual times. We are living in critical days. The enemy is aggressive, but the Kingdom is advancing—and God is raising up a people of unshakable faith.

This message isn't just for you. It's for those around you. Your family. Your church. Your city. Your future.

Don't settle for good when God has called you to great. Don't let fear rob you another day. Don't wait for better circumstances. Faith changes your circumstances.

Build your faith. Confess the Word. Act on it and watch what God will do. This is your moment. This is your faith. This is your time.

Faith Study Journal

How to Use This Journal

This journal is designed to help you internalize and apply each chapter from "Faith That Moves the World." Each section contains reflection prompts, Scripture study, confession writing, and faith action planning. Go at your own pace but maintain consistency. Faith grows through use.

Chapter 1: Why Does Faith Matter?

Scriptures to Study:

- Matthew 8:5–13
- Matthew 9:27–31
- Hebrews 11:1–6
- 1 John 5:4, Ephesians 2:8

Reflect:

Why is faith essential in the Kingdom of God?

_____

_____

_____

_____

_____

What stood out to you about how Jesus responded to faith?

_____

_____

_____

_____

Write It:

What does it mean for you personally that "faith is how we overcome"?

_____

_____

_____

_____

Declare It:

Write a confession based on one of the Scriptures above.

_____

_____

_____

_____

Faith in Action:

What area of your life do you need to respond in faith instead of waiting in fear?

_____

_____

_____

_____

Chapter 2: What Is Faith—and What It's Not

Scriptures to Study:

- Hebrews 11:1
- Romans 4:17–21
- 2 Corinthians 5:7
- Romans 10:17

Reflect:

How would you define faith in your own words?

_____

_____

_____

_____

_____

Have you ever realized you were operating in head faith instead of heart faith?

_____

_____

_____

_____

_____

Write It:

What are some things you need to stop "feeling out" and start "faithing through"?

_____

_____

_____

_____

_____

Declare It:

"I walk by faith and not by sight. I believe without needing to see. God's Word is final."

Faith in Action:

List a step you can take this week to trust God beyond your senses.

_____

_____

_____

_____

_____

Chapter 3: Where Does Faith Come From?

Scriptures to Study:

- Romans 10:17, Proverbs 4:20–22, Romans 4:20–21

Reflect:

What voices are currently shaping your faith or fear?

_____
_____
_____
_____

How are you prioritizing the Word in your daily routine?

_____
_____
_____
_____
_____

Write It:

How can you shift your attention back to the Word?

_____
_____
_____
_____
_____

Declare It:

"My focus is on the Word of God. My faith is growing daily."

Faith in Action:

- Schedule your Word time daily and stick to it this week.

Chapter 4: Building Your Faith

Scriptures to Study:

- Joshua 1:6–9, Mark 4:13–20, Luke 17:5–6

Reflect:

Have you been meditating on the Word or just reading it?

_____

_____

_____

_____

What's one verse you want to take deeper this week?

_____

_____

_____

_____

_____

Write It:

What does your faith "root system" look like?

_____

_____

_____

_____

_____

Declare It:

"My roots are going deep. I'm not shaken. I'm standing strong."

Faith in Action:

- Choose one verse to meditate on all week. Write it down and repeat it daily.

Chapter 5: Fear—Faith's Enemy

Scriptures to Study:

- Mark 4:13–20, Proverbs 23:7, Numbers 13–14

Reflect:

What thoughts or voices have been feeding fear in your life?

_____

_____

_____

_____

_____

Are you "faith in reverse" in any area?

_____

_____

_____

_____

_____

Write It:

Identify a fear-based mindset and write a Scripture-based truth to replace it.

_____

_____

_____

_____

_____

Declare It:

"I reject fear. I walk by faith. God's Word is the final authority over my life."

Faith in Action:

- Confront one fear this week with bold action and declaration.

Chapter 6: Working Your Faith

Scriptures to Study:

- Habakkuk 2:4
- Romans 1:17
- Galatians 3:11
- Hebrews 10:38
- Mark 11:22–24

Reflect:

Are you actively working your faith or just holding beliefs?

_____

_____

_____

_____

_____

Where do you need to put faith into motion?

_____

_____

_____

_____

_____

Write It:

What promise do you need to stand on with conviction and action?

_____

_____

_____

_____

_____

Declare It:

"My faith is alive. I believe, I speak, and I act in line with the Word."

Faith in Action:

- Take one bold action that lines up with what you believe.

Chapter 7: Head vs. Heart Faith

Scriptures to Study:

- John 20:24–29
- Romans 4:17–21
- Proverbs 3:5–6

Reflect:

Are there truths you agree with mentally but haven't trusted in your heart?

_____

_____

_____

_____

_____

What keeps faith from dropping from your head to your heart?

_____

_____

_____

_____

_____

Write It:

Describe a time when head faith failed—but heart faith could have changed the outcome.

_____

_____

_____

_____

_____

Declare It:

"I live by heart faith. I believe God beyond my senses. His Word is rooted in me."

Faith in Action:

- Spend time meditating on one promise until it goes from head knowledge to heart conviction.

Chapter 8: Releasing Your Faith

Scriptures to Study:

- Mark 5:25–29
- Romans 10:10
- Hebrews 3:1
- 2 Corinthians 4:13

Reflect:

What are you believing for but not speaking or acting on?

_____

_____

_____

_____

_____

Are your words aligning with your faith?

_____

_____

_____

_____

_____

Write It:

Write a bold, Scripture-based confession over your current situation.

_____

_____

_____

_____

_____

Declare It:

"I release my faith with my words. I call things that be not as though they were."

Faith in Action:

- Start each day this week with your confession and act on it.

Chapter 9: Faith in the Final Hour

Scriptures to Study:

- 2 Timothy 3:1–5
- Matthew 24:13
- Hebrews 11:7

Reflect:

How does your faith prepare you for the days we're living in?

_____

_____

_____

_____

_____

Are you letting the world shape your faith—or letting your faith shape the world?

_____

_____

_____

_____

_____

Write It:

What does it look like to live boldly by faith in this final hour?

_____

_____

_____

_____

_____

Declare It:

"My faith is built for this hour. I am part of God's remnant. I will not back down."

Faith in Action:

- Encourage someone else to stand in faith this week. Share what you've learned.

Chapter 10: Activate Your Faith

Scriptures to Study:

- James 1:22
- Matthew 7:24–27
- Mark 11:23–24
- Joshua 6:2–20

Reflect:

Where do you need to stop waiting and start acting?

_____

_____

_____

_____

_____

What step of faith are you afraid to take?

_____

_____

_____

_____

_____

Write It:

Create a personal "faith plan" based on one area of your life:

What you believe

_____

_____

_____

_____

_____

What you will confess

_____

_____

_____

_____

_____

What you will do

_____

_____

_____

_____

_____

Declare It:

"I activate my faith. I am a doer of the Word. I walk in victory."

Faith in Action:

- Take that step. Don't wait. Do what the Word says— and expect results.

Use this journal daily, weekly, or alongside your Bible study. Faith comes by hearing—but grows by doing. Teach it. Live it. And move the world with it.

Do You Know Jesus?

Jesus loves you!

If you're depressed, he can give you joy to the full. If you're troubled, he can give you peace.

You may have started out going the wrong way, but you don't have to keep going that way. You can choose Christ now and get on the right track.

There's not one issue God can't answer for you. You are only one decision away from God turning your life around for the better. No one has ever come to Jesus, and their life got worse; their life always got better.

What do you need to do?

1. Repent toward Jesus and away from sin.

2. Confess Jesus as Lord and Savior

3. Receive Jesus by faith and live committed to His teaching.

Why not give your life to Christ now? The Bible tells us that God is not willing that any should perish, but that all should come to repentance.

Pray this prayer:

Dear Heavenly Father,
Thank you for your Son Jesus Christ. Jesus…thank you for coming and dying on the cross for me. I confess you TODAY as Lord and Savior of my life. Come into my heart and cleanse me of all my sin. Connect me to my new beginning. I believe you are alive, that God raised you up. I declare that you are the King of Kings and Lord of Lords. In Jesus' name I have prayed. AMEN!

Congratulations on the best decision of your life! I have had regrets, but choosing Jesus was never one of them. Welcome to your best life.

If you prayed this prayer, please let me know. Email me: HLCC@LIVE.CA

- Get into a good church.
- Find yourself a Bible and read it daily.
- Talk to God every day.
- Tell others about the hope you found in Christ.

About the Author

Philip Hutchings' passion and love for God and God's Word connect to his desire to be used in bringing in the final harvest of souls on the Earth today and see the worldwide church in revival. After graduating from Zion Bible College in Barrington, R.I. in 2004, Philip has encouraged and helped many men, women, and children of many nationalities. The unique delivery of the spoken Word through Philip has released the power of God to see transformation in many lives. Philip and his wife Jamie felt impressed of the Lord to birth a church in Saint John, New Brunswick, Canada called Higher Life Church, and he continues to pastor and minister with his team. After going to jail and being put into solitary confinement for seven days for refusing to close the church during COVID, God has given him a national platform to preach the Gospel and see hope restored in the Church across Canada.

facebook.com/higherlifecanada
x.com/HLChurchCanada

www.ingramcontent.com/pod-product-compliance
Lightning Source LLC
LaVergne TN
LVHW051427080426
835508LV00022B/3278